Historic Strikes and Their Settlement; Also, Fundamentals of Street-car Control

PART I

HISTORIC STRIKES
AND
THEIR SETTLEMENT

BEING AN ACCOUNT OF

LABOR'S GREAT BATTLES IN AMERICA,
HOW THEY BEGAN AND ENDED,
WHAT SOLDIERS AND CITI-
ZENS HAVE DONE
TO MAKE
PEACE

—— ALSO ——

A REVIEW OF ANCIENT LABOR TROUBLES

BY

LEIGH H. IRVINE

THE CALKINS NEWSPAPER SYNDICATE
24 CLAY STREET, SAN FRANCISCO
—1907—

THE MASSES SUFFER.

The fates of the great majority have ever been, and doubtless still are, so sad that it is painful to think of them. Unquestionably the existing type of social organization is one which none who care for their kind can contemplate with satisfaction; and unquestionably men's actiyities accompanying this type are far from being admirable. The strong divisions of rank and the immense inequalities of means are at variance with that ideal of human relations on which the sympathetic imagination likes to dwell; and the average conduct, under the pressure and excitement of social life as at present carried on, is in sundry respects repulsive. Herbert Spencer, on page 4 of "A Plea for Liberty."

NOT SOCIALISM.

There is no Socialism in recognizing the plain fact that the gifts of fortune are not distributed in this world according to merit. There is no Socialism in declaring that the rich, by reason of their riches, have responsibilities towards the poor; or that the poor, by reason of their poverty, have claims upon the rich. Nor is there any Socialism in holding that the State has responsibilities toward the poor, and that the law ought, when necessary, to assert the reasonable claims of poverty, and enforce the reasonable duties and obligations of wealth. John Rae, page 9 of "Contemporary Socialism."

BISMARCK'S VIEWS.

If you do not cry out about State Socialism whenever the State does anything for the laborer in the way of Christian charity—then you will destroy the charm of social democracy. Bismarck, quoted on page 421 of Rae's "Contemporary Socialism."

DANGER AHEAD.

It was de Toqueville's theory ("Democracy in America") that "free institutions run continual risk of shipwreck when power is the possession of the many, but property—from whatever cause—the possession of the few. With the advance of democracy a diffusion of wealth becomes almost a necessity of State."

INTRODUCTION.

IN 1902 I hurriedly visited Yuma, Arizona, where I met for the first and last time the eminent C. Osborne Ward, author of "Ancient Lowly." The great savant lay dying, one of his comprehensive literary plans unfinished.

As a young man he had studied with the immortal Darwin, had worked with Schliemann among the ruins of ancient Troy, and had served our Federal Government with distinction for a quarter of a century, his field being in the Department of Labor. His "Ancient Lowly" had then been recognized for many years as the ablest book on early social conditions, and it stands to-day as the monumental achievement of a long and scholarly life, much of which was devoted to original investigation in history and economics.

As I had devoted many years to both field and academic service in the study of social and economic problems, and had collaborated with Mr. Ward in an undertaking only then fairly started, he appointed me his literary executor to carry out some of his plans, these to be designed in part from notes which he gave to me as he neared the end.

During the extensive research incident to carrying out the departed scholar's unfinished volumes—not yet completed by me—I have made a careful study of both ancient and modern labor conditions. It is for these reasons, in part, that I venture, not immodestly I hope, to offer this brief history of some of the important battles of organized labor, together with a slight account of the struggles of the lowly classes of antiquity.

In these days of vexatious labor troubles, many thoughtful citizens wonder whether the present economic system is about to be overthrown by violence. Thousands of prudent men and women fear for the future, feeling that, as one writer has said, "Foreign hordes of anarchists, masquerading as labor-unionists, are organizing to destroy American liberty."

A careful study of the industrial wars of thirty years convinces me that the red-shirted anarchist, loud-mouthed and blatant, is as much despised by the honest leaders of labor as by the conservative "captains of industry" who own the great bulk of the wealth of the land.

Despite many regrettable evils in the unions, and though violence and bloodshed have often accompanied strikes, it will be found, on the whole, that both employer and employee have grown steadily more liberal and tolerant than they were, for example, in 1877, also that the wiser national leaders of labor federations **know that violence spells defeat.**

The public at large, that great body of non-combatants that always suffers more than the belligerents, has in recent years **made insistent demands for peace,** and the spirit of conciliation has often pervaded the ranks of the warring forces, even against their will, society at large **demanding with increasing emphasis** that the duelists in the "affairs of honor" between employer and employee must desist from clogging the wheels of industry while they do slaughter in the public streets. For these reasons, rather than because of the handling of rioters by police, militia, and Federal soldiers, **the lesson of history reveals the victories of society,** the great umpire, **the court whose mandates neither capital nor labor dare permanently to defy.** Vast progress has been made during the era between the "Molly Maguire" outrages, for example, and that of the Roosevelt Arbitration Board, which settled a gigantic coal strike that threatened to assault the very foundations of government.

In the ancient mines of Laurium the laborer, who was believed to have no soul, was chained to his task in underground pest-holes where each day's work only enlarged his tomb. In these modern days of closer relationship between the hired man and his employer each battle settled by calmness and the spirit of conciliation increases the respect of the contestants for each other and enlarges, not the tomb of the slave, as in ancient Laurium, but the field of life and opportunity for the sons of toil.

LEIGH H. IRVINE.

24 Clay Street, San Francisco, May, 1907.

ANCIENT LABOR TROUBLES.

I have but one lamp by which my feet are guided, and that is the lamp of experience. I know of no way of judging of the future but by the past.—**Patrick Henry.**

THOSE who believe that labor troubles are of modern origin belong to the class that deny that the earth rotates on its axis. It is well known that the primal condition of man, so far as we have gone in historic research, was that of master and slave, of brutality and rebellion.

The workers of antiquity were involved in frequent and bitter strifes that resulted from unions for the betterment of the masses. Laborers of the Roman Empire, under Constantine, had about thirty-five unions, and seven hundred years before the Christian era, according to Plutarch, Mommsen, and Ward, trade-unions existed in great numbers. Numa Pompilius granted the unions freedom from hostile legislation, and Tarquin and Claudius were unable to stamp them out. Cicero led the aristocrats in denouncing labor organizations, but they were not put down. Solon, the great law-giver of Athens, recognized and made laws for the unions. The Solonic Dispensation is famous in history.

Artisans in the building trades maintained their organizations during six hundred years at Rome, and for about as long in Attica and other parts of Greece. Organization permeated almost every branch of industry, including the circus performers, gladiators, and fortune-tellers. Pagan image-makers objected to Christianity because it would destroy the trade of godsmithing, which employed an army of skilful idol-makers.

The first great historic strike was that of Moses and the Jews, known as the Exodus. This was strangely like modern strikes. The Hebrews sought in vain to induce the Egyptians to modify the hard tasks imposed upon them. Many bloody conflicts took place between masters and servants, but Moses organized the workers and achieved freedom. Moses ordered not far from a million Hebrew workers to throw down their implements of toil and march away. It was physical and economic as well as religious causes that induced the two great brothers—Moses and Aaron—to petition King Pharaoh for relief from overwork, bad food, and injustice. The king was sour and insulting, saying, ''Wherefore do ye lead the people from their work?'' History records the fact that the great strike of Moses—a rebellion, in fact—led up to the Law of Moses, for the author had then become both statesman and deliverer.

Another noted strike grew out of the Eleusinian Mysteries, held at Eleusis, about ten miles from Athens. It was customary for the Eleusinian devotees to give up to their festivities nine days every five years. They were insulted and assaulted by crusading slaves and laborers, who struck against exclusion from religious rites in the Eleusinian Mysteries. The strikers, descended from generations of skilful artisans, had built the magnificent palaces and temples of Greece. As their skill had been recognized and celebrated, they felt that their personality and their union should not be spurned. Their outbreak was the forerunner of battles that brought greater freedom to the laborers of those eras of bloodshed and brutality.

Another great battle was led by Nabis, a genius and leader of workingmen. He fought the Ephori, who were five secret despots of ancient Greece. The Ephori trained young aristocrats in the art of assassinating laborers, teaching the hot-blooded aristocrats to be ready at any moment, with daggers, to butcher the naked, half-starved and unarmed working classes in sufficient number to keep down the labor forces to a schedule made by the Ephori. Nabis made an ancient French Revolution of the situation, invented engines of devilism—stabbing manikins, broadaxes, death-traps—and when his labor hordes and he had finished their bloody work the Ephori had sunk, never to rise again. Nabis careered 207 years B. C.

One of the most wonderful uprisings of ancient labor was 413 B. C., when 20,000 chained slaves working in the silver mines of Laurium, where men and women, painted and naked, seldom saw the light of day, bolted for the Spartan garrison, and aided the brave Spartans in their twenty-seven years' war against the Athenians. This strike was a heavy blow to the Athenians, who not only lost the slave miners and armor-makers, but beheld their former slaves, rewarded by new masters, fighting against them bitterly in the war that defeated and humbled Athens. This strike cost Athens her prestige. But Laurium furnished yet another strike.

The worker in the Laurium silver mines—B. C. 133—was the lowest kind of a slave. He was usually a prisoner of war. The mines—thirty miles from Athens—were foul subterranean caverns in which the naked and painted laborer was chained and put to work himself to death under the direction of savage masters who had leased the slave from the Empire.

One day the striking miners killed their overseers, robbed the armories, and took the town. They laid waste the country, but were finally defeated by Heraklitos, the mayor, "when the usual brutalities of wholesale crucifixion ensued and nearly all the miners were put to death."

At Latium—194 B. C.—a strike of slaves was caused by a lockout. Combining with the labor slaves of the city, a horde of degraded and impoverished agricultural workers got up a strike during a gala day when the inhabitants of Setia, a village, were about to witness gladiatorial contests. A traitor betrayed the strikers, whereupon Merula, the praetor, led the trained troops of Rome into the field, and two thousand strikers were put to death.

There were many bloody strikes hundreds of years before as well as after Christ. One is a typical example of conditions. On the island of Scio (ancient Chios), seven miles from the coast of Asia Minor, slavery existed in diabolical forms. About two hundred and fifty years A. D. a slave named Drimakos led a number of deserters to mountain fastnesses, where he became their king. The rich Chians were defeated in trying to capture the slave leader and his men.

In a conference with the city magistrates Drimakos induced them to sign a treaty. He said: "What we want is subsistence, no more; but we will never again submit to drudgery or bondage." The compact was lived up to until the Chians plotted to have Drimakos murdered, whereupon the great leader, hearing of the plot, induced his favorite young man to anticipate the Chians in their desire for his head. He said: "Son, to him that bringeth my head the Chians offer money and freedom. I have lived long enough; thou art dear to me, therefore thy duty is to cut off my head, take it to them, receive thy reward, return home, and be happy."

Reluctantly the young man obeyed, but Drimakos's band

ravaged the country, tortured the Chians, and built a monument to Drimakos, their hero.

Prominent among the great battles of ancient labor is that wherein the immortal Spartacus led the strike of the gladiators' union, saying: "If ye are men, strike down yon guard, follow me, and gain the mountain passes. If ye are beasts, stand there like fat oxen waiting for the butcher's knife." This speech is supposed to have been made about 75 B. C.

Aided by slaves and unions Spartacus dealt many hard blows to Rome, showing himself a brave general and a genius, exceedingly humane for his age. Dissensions and jealousies among his followers probably resulted in his undoing. After many notable victories that terrified Rome from 74 to 70 B. C., Spartacus and most of his men were slaughtered in a battle unwisely forced into by his restless followers. Six thousand of his men escaped, but they were captured and crucified along the Appian Way. Workingmen were then persecuted with great severity until the doctrines of Christ came to teach the brotherhood of man.

Florus says Spartacus died like a Roman emperor, killing scores and falling with his body so completely cut to shreds that it was never identified. The Romans then gave no quarter, but killed sixty thousand workingmen "who died in a defeat that caused the chains of labor to be more securely riveted for ages."

STRIKES IN THE UNITED STATES.

In the year 1881 there were 471 strikes in the United States, and in 1900 there were 1779. Between the years 1881 and 1900 there were 22,793 strikes. During this era the strikes ordered by labor organizations culminated thus: Succeeded, 52.86 per cent; partly succeeded, 13.60 per cent; failed, 33.54 per cent. Of the strikes not ordered, 55.39 per cent failed.—**Census Reports.**

The history of strikes during the last half century has accentuated four facts: (1) The losses to the strikers have been much exaggerated. The permanent gain from a successful strike often outweighs the temporary loss of all strikes, including the failures. The **real injury** is the disarrangement of industry and its effect on the consumer. (2) With the growth of unionism there has been a distinct improvement in the conduct of strikes. Violence and bloodshed are now less common than formerly. (3) The oldest unions approve of strikes only as a last resort. * * * Unionism has been on the whole a conservative force. (4) The outcome of a strike is largely dependent on the state of public opinion, and the strike itself is no longer held to be a matter of private concern between the employer and the workmen. The coal strike of

1902 was won, and the New York Subway strike of 1905 was lost, almost entirely because the issues were so clear that the general public sentiment favored the strikers in the one case and opposed them in the other.—**Professor Seligman, of Columbia University, pages 439 and 440 of Principles of Economics.**

OF THE many thousands of strikes that have disturbed the public peace of the United States, or parts of it, within the last thirty years, only a few have been of that far-reaching character and general scope to warrant their classification as of historic importance.

Though it is common to hear all sorts of predictions of general revolution, if one chances to be in the vortex of a local labor storm, the truth is that the thousand or two strikes that embroil employers and employees each year throughout the United States are mostly of local significance, though they may show the existence of a widespread economic disease.

Glancing rapidly at old strikes in America, that of the bakers of New York, in 1741, is probably the oldest of which we have any record. It was followed by disturbances of some importance in Philadelphia, in 1796, and again in 1798. The shoemakers were the workers involved, and they called their battle a 'turnout.' This strike lasted ten weeks; it was for an increase of wages, and it was partly successful.

One of the most notable of the early strikes was that of the sailors. It occurred in New York in 1803. The sailors marched and forced others to join them in their demand for more pay. They were pursued by constables, arrested, and lodged in jail. Their strike failed.

In 1805 the shoemakers of Philadelphia went on a six weeks' strike for increased wages. Though they were prosecuted for conspiracy, there is no record of their conviction, and there is evidence that they won their point.

In November, 1809, the cordwainers of New York struck, and for the first time the disturbance was called a **strike.** They were defeated. It was they who invented the word 'scab,' which they then applied to non-union men.

During 1817 at Medford, Massachusetts, Thacher Magoun, a shipbuilder, precipitated a strike by abolishing the grog privilege from his shipyard. "No rum" signs were plastered all over his works, whereupon the men rebelled, but they finally gave in, and a ship was finished without the use of liquor. This is probably the first strike and the last ever instituted for reasons that would please a prohibitionist.

The year 1835 was fairly free from labor troubles, though five hundred mechanics in Boston struck for a ten-hour day, as did a few hundred men in a score of mills at Paterson, New Jersey.

The stonecutters of New York struck during the same year for an increase of wages, and for regulation of piece-work. It is interesting to note that during this time the merchants of Schuylkill pledged themselves to employ no laborers except such as would agree to work from sunrise until sunset. During the same year there was a strike in the Philadelphia coal yards. About this time several branches of workmen in Philadelphia marched the streets with banners, demanding that they be compelled to work "from six to six only."

About this period there were various strikes, some successful, of carpenters, tinplate and sheetiron workers, cordwainers, tailors, tailoresses, bookbinders, folders, and others. The master bookbinders resolved to increase women's wages to $3 a week, declaring less than that sum "inhuman and oppressive."

There was no time or inclination for strikes during the Civil War, but from 1870 on to 1877 there was considerable trouble. Coal miners, railroad employees, and others, strove hard to get more pay.

Carroll D. Wright, late United States Commissioner of Labor, found that there were 1741 strikes and lockouts between the years 1741 and 1880. Of that number only 316 succeeded. One hundred and fifty-four were compromised, and 583 completely failed. In 438 cases reports are not to be obtained. In 1089 cases the contention was over wages. In 1880 there were 610 strikes, but prior to that there had not been to exceed eighty or ninety a year. Mr. Wright thinks that statistics will show, when finally compiled, that there has been a decrease in the total number of strikes during the years following 1900.

The First Great Modern Strike.

The first of modern historic strikes was one of momentous importance and serious culmination. It was on the Baltimore and Ohio Railroad, at Martinsburg, West Virginia, and news of its progress caused great alarm in the public mind, for the many outrages of the anarchistic organization known as the "Molly Maguires," in the anthracite coal regions of Pennsylvania, had caused many persons to fear that the Molly Maguires, working in secret with deadly purpose, meant to kill the rich, destroy property, and bring about "the dreadful equality of the unequal." The Maguires had been very active in the perpetration of tragedies during the late sixties. In fact, however, the Molly Maguires never started an open strike. They were terrorists and desperadoes.

Coming back to the first historic strike—that on the Baltimore and Ohio system—the immediate cause of the trouble was a cut of ten per cent in wages, coupled with irregular employment, long runs, the separation of men from their families by having 'layoffs' at inconvenient, expensive, and distant points, and some other grievances, such as withholding men's pay for three or four months. It is easy to imagine the bitterness that such abuses engendered.

The state militia at Martinsburg and Pittsburg sympathized with and refused to fire on the strikers. At Cincinnati, Toledo, St. Louis, Syracuse, Buffalo, Chicago, and elsewhere there were riots. This strike wore itself out, but better conditions followed for both employer and employee.

Another remarkable strike was that on the Pennsylvania Railroad in 1877. After the panic of 1873 the road reduced wages, and again in June, 1877. The employees of the roads having terminals at Pittsburg formed the Trainmen's Union and decided to strike at noon, June 27. Though it involved many roads and branches, the storm center was at Allegheny City and Pittsburg. Owing to poor organization and the work of a traitor who informed the Company what the men were doing, this strike did not become a very bloody one. On July 19, however, the storm broke in earnest. Though the trainmen engaging were not authorized by the Trainmen's Union, and though that organization was not to blame, yet the mobs increased, the strikers increasing in number and violence. On the 20th of July they had reached to the number of five thousand, and on the 21st they gave battle to the troops of Pennsylvania infantry. The guns of the militia were seized, the bayonets twisted off, and the troops did not have any power over the mobs. Twenty-two persons were killed by shots, stones, or volleys from the troops.

When the troops rested for food the mobs formed again, and as the rioters had by that time broken into gun stores and armed themselves they were prepared for an earnest fight. Cars were burned, the roundhouse was set on fire, and a field-piece was obtained by the mob. Attacks were frequent until the 23d. Despite the soldiers and a citizens' committee cars were fired, thugs and thieves fell in line as camp-followers, and before the end was in sight sixteen hundred cars, one hundred and twenty-six locomotives, and all the shops and buildings of the Company had been destroyed. Tracks were torn up or ruined by fire. The damage reached $5,000,000, and a judgment for $3,592,789 was rendered against the county of Allegheny. The last of this debt was paid by the county in 1906.

The Telegraphers' Battle.

The next great strike was a quiet one compared with the one just described. It was the revolt of the telegraphers, in 1883. The men wanted the cessation of Sunday work without pay, wanted eight-hour days, and the equalization of pay between men and women. A demand was also made for increase of wages. This strike failed, lasting from July 19 to August 23, and the employees lost a quarter of a million dollars.

The Gould-System Strike.

In 1885 and 1886 there was a great strike on the Southwestern or Gould System of railways. The first outbreak was at Sedalia, Missouri, March 7, 1885, but on the 17th of March work was resumed.

In March, 1886, the Knights of Labor ordered a strike on the Gould System because a foreman prominent in the order had been discharged. For nearly a month the business of the road was paralyzed, and the strike was declared off. The Company would not thereafter treat with its men, except individually. The strike was therefore renewed on April 5, but its backbone had been broken, the public was not with the men, and they lost.

Homesteaders Kill Pinkertons.

The next great battle was in July, 1892, when much trouble arose between the Carnegie Steel Company and its men at Homestead, Pennsylvania. No agreement could be reached regarding wages, and on June 30 the Company closed its works and discharged its men. The men for the most part were members of the Amalgamated Association of Iron and Steel Workers, and though the immediate question then at issue involved but a few of the Carnegie workmen, yet the Amalgamated affiliation caused the trouble. **The union men resolved to prevent the opening of the works with non-union men.**

On July 4 the union men prevented the sheriff and his deputies from guarding the works and aiding non-union men to work. Later two barges loaded with Pinkerton detectives approached on the Ohio River. The strikers hid behind piles of steel billets, from which they fired on the detectives and prevented them from landing. Though armed with Winchester rifles, the Pinkertons were prevented from landing. They were again and again driven to their boats, many being killed. This was on July 5.

On July 6 the strikers, having obtained a brass cannon, commanded the barges. Another force of a thousand strikers got a cannon and took up a position on the opposite side of the river, where a breastwork of railroad ties was thrown up. The boats were fired on for hours, but they were protected by steel plates, and many barrels of oil were thrown into the river in an attempt to fire the boats. The Pinkertons waved a flag of truce and surrendered. Seven Pinkertons had been killed, twenty-three wounded. On their march through the streets, after surrender, the survivors of the Pinkertons were treated with much abuse.

On July 10 the Governor sent the entire force of the militia to Homestead, and on the 12th Homestead was placed under martial law and peace was restored. Congress investigated the affair, but no legislative action ever resulted. The strike was not declared off until November, 1892. It was one of the bitterest of all labor's wars.

The Pullman Strike of 1894.

There is now a general belief among labor leaders that the great Pullman strike, ordered May 11, 1894, might have been avoided by the exercise of good judgment. The reason for this decision is that the original controversy involved men who were not railway employees, and that the American Railway Union, a transitory sort of organization, which had won a victory over the Great Northern Railroad, erred in taking the Pullman employees into its membership. It should be said that the A. R. U. did not advise the strike, but it felt that it had to stand by the local Pullman men in their battle.

In anticipation of a lockout of the Pullman men the A. R. U. ordered the strike, boycotted Pullman cars, and involved the country in a great strike. The American Federation of Labor refused to order a sympathetic strike, but the A. R. U. carried on the battle alone, with a great accompaniment of riots, murder, and other crimes. United States troops were here and there on the scene to protect Federal property, particularly at Chicago. Altogether nearly fifteen thousand troops were engaged, not to quell the strike, but to protect property.

The A. R. U. numbered about one hundred and fifty thousand members during the Pullman strike, and the controversy assumed an intensely bitter form, the Union holding practically that the public had no rights in the controversy, and that the Union might paralyze business if necessary to maintain its existence. It should here be said that the courts, not the army, broke this strike, which ceased about July 15. Injunctions against the strikers were numerous in the Federal courts.

The railroads lost $5,000,000 in earnings, the strikers at Pullman, numbering 3100, lost $350,000 in wages, and 100,000 or more employees of roads centering at Chicago lost $1,500,000 in wages. Bradstreets puts the public loss at $80,000,000. The A. R. U. attempted to destroy the great railway brotherhoods in retaliation for their failure to give aid, but the A. R. U. itself perished, while the brotherhoods survive, stronger than ever, being recognized and respected by railroad managers.

The Anthracite Strike.

One of the marvelous results of conciliation is seen in the anthracite coal strike of 1900, which resulted in an increase of ten per cent in coal miners' wages. The coal barons settled for political and business reasons, but felt sour and vindictive. For these reasons there was good temper for a big battle in 1902, when the United Mine Workers of America asked for an increase of wages and a decrease of time. Really there was a deeper grievance. The men wanted recognition, but the operators were firm in withholding it.

After many failures, through conferences and otherwise, one hundred and forty-seven thousand miners threw up their jobs and were idle from May 12 to October 23, 1902.

The coal mining companies were short $46,000,000 in coal receipts during the strike, the men lost $25,000,000 in wages, and $1,800,000 was spent by mine workers throughout the United States for the relief of their striking brethren. · Railroad companies probably lost $50,000,000 in freights.

Despite the Union's protest against violence and appeal for peaceful measures, there were boycotts, murders, and general violence.

On October 3 President Roosevelt arranged a conference of the coal barons and the principal officers of the Mine Workers of America, but nothing definite was done. This caused great apprehension in business circles, and there was widespread fear of grave trouble, such as the bread riots that have often occurred in England.

Suddenly the operators asked the President to appoint a commission, pledging themselves to abide by its decision. The union miners, on request of the President, consented to abide by the award of the Presidential Commission. This stopped the strike at once, and for five months the Commission took evidence and heard the parties to the controversy. The award was finally made and signed by employers and employees. The agreement was to continue in full force for three years, and its terms were respected. By getting together the parties to the controversy learned more about each other, and better feeling has prevailed ever since.

Colorado Disturbances.

There were severe Colorado disturbances in 1903, involving four of the fifty-nine counties of the State. There had been trouble for many years among the miners, and at Cripple Creek there were great outbreaks in 1903-04. The miners deported non-union men, and the Citizens' Alliance retaliated by deporting union men. Murders, boycotts, imprisonments, and injunctions followed. During fourteen years the State spent more than $1,000,000 for military campaigns to quell riots. The last of these grave troubles was in June, 1904, but the effects of none of them have really been of national importance. It is now known that the most violent and lawless labor-union men in the country infested the Colorado districts, going later to Nevada to continue their work of tearing down and disrupting society.

Other Strikes.

Early in 1906 it was seen that the year would be one of defeat for labor. In the case of the larger strikes the unions met with grave repulses, because their strikes were unwise, and in most cases they were not approved by national labor organizations. Early in the year a six-months' strike in the Fall River, Massachusetts, cotton mills was settled through the mediation of Governor Douglas, and later a second battle was avoided by the raising of operatives' wages. In March a strike on the Subway and the elevated roads of New York was easily defeated in six days, as it was not approved by national organizations of employees, which have often proved a conservative influence.

Chicago Teamsters.

One of the long, bitter, and disastrous strikes of recent times was that of the Chicago teamsters, May to July 20, 1905, which was attended by great violence. It began as a sympathetic strike to aid garment workers who had practically lost their strike before the teamsters sought to aid them. Nineteen persons were killed, and several hundred were wounded during the battles that accompanied this war. The teamsters were finally defeated, never having had public approval. Some persons close to the scene, reporters and other observers, have said that this was the most foolish, corrupt, and cruel of recent strikes; others have even charged that it was managed in the interest of competing companies who corrupted several labor leaders. Jurors, editors, and investigators now agree that there was corruption on both sides. In other strikes at Chicago it has been charged that the unions and their employers have now and then combined to rob the public.

Unions to Remain.

In 1905 President Roosevelt, in his annual message to Congress, declared for the second time that, in his opinion, trade-unions have come to stay, and that they must be dealt with as permanent factors. He recommended legislation concerning child labor, the work of women, and germane matters.

Reduced Efficiency.

Some of the strongest union men are planning to increase the efficiency of labor. They recognize the fact that every time a union "lets down the bars" and brings in non-union competitors, after their surrender, the standard of efficiency is lowered, and that a union card is no longer what it was in the old days—a badge of competency. In other words, the increased union membership, recruited largely from incompetents of the surrendering 'scab' class, is not the membership that would come under strict conditions in times of industrial peace.

Elements of Weakness.

There are several practices that make for weakness in labor organizations, one of the principal ones being the limitation of apprentices. In seeking to prevent a surplus of journeymen in the various trades, unions curtail the number of those who are permitted to learn trades. If a young man wants to learn this or that trade he is confronted by prohibitory rules that forbid the teaching of more than a limited number of apprentices, wherefore the cry that unions of foreigners prevent American youth from mastering trades. In some quarters this feature has alienated many citizens from sympathy with unionism.

In Pittsburg a few years ago it was discovered that a mechanic who insisted on doing practically as much work in eight hours as he had formerly done in nine was "knocked in the head" and otherwise assaulted until he agreed to curtail his output. Many similar instances have been reported, lately a case in Oakland, California. It is the opinion of some of the shrewdest union men that the barring of American youth from the opportunities of life, and the tyrannical curtailment of work, coupled with the growing inefficiency of union men, sound the death knell of the unionism of to-day. Others, among them students of marked ability, foresee a reformation of abuses and the strengthening rather than the disintegration of unionism.

Recent Decisions.

In some recent English cases, and in one celebrated case in Connecticut, individual members of unions were sued with the union as an organization for damages inflicted by violent strikers. Heavy judgments were rendered and enforced against the defendants. It is the opinion of Carroll D. Wright that such cases will act as deterrent forces, modifying both the number and severity of strikes. Some of the more conservative union leaders believe the decisions have been a benefit to their cause, tending to correct abuses and prevent violence.

Noted Settlements.

Vice-president Baldwin, of the Southern Railway (1895), treated with the six thousand employees operating over the four thousand miles of the system. The men were growing weary of the reduction of wages that had been in force since 1893. After conferring for some days, examining receipts and expenses, and investigating all the facts submitted by Vice-president Baldwin, the men were entirely satisfied, and there was no strike. Some little points of friction were adjusted, and conciliation left all parties feeling friendly. Capitalists recognized Baldwin's ability and gave him the presidency of a vast enterprise, and labor has since built a monument to his memory. His far-sighted policy, coupled with high ideals along the line of the Golden Rule, furnish a wonderful object-lesson for the emulation of other captains and privates of industry.

Former Mayor Abram S. Hewitt, of New York, was once met by his men from the 'works,' which had been running at a loss. Wages had not been satisfactory for a long time, and the men were chafing under a reduction of ten per cent, therefore they demanded more money.

"Boys, send in an auditor and examine our books," said the Mayor, and they did so. The result was they withdrew their demand, and offered to stand a further cut of ten per cent, but Mr. Hewitt rejected the invitation. The old Mayor used to laugh, after that, and say, "Do you think you could get up a strike in our works now?" His policy, like Baldwin's, resulted in industrial peace and "good understanding" thereafter.

Strikes to End.

Carroll D. Wright, for many years United States Commissioner of Labor, and a careful student of every phase of industrial troubles, says he realizes that the era of strikes is passing away, or will pass away, adding: "I believe that the good sense of the workingmen of this country, co-operating with the good sense and wisdom of the employers of labor, will see to it that strikes do not occur and that the public is not inconvenienced. All strikes are uneconomic in their results, but the strike problem can not be solved by courts, by laws, by military force, or by any drastic measure."

Light Ahead.

A study of the evolution of industry, a growth always accompanied by the multiplication of trades that demand culture, gives hope of a brighter industrial future than most men ever picture.

Poverty is no new thing. It was old at ancient Nippur, and Nippur was old almost ten thousand years before Christ. Coming to modern eras and conditions, one need do no more than read Macaulay's "History of England" for vivid and accurate accounts of the pauperism and famine that confronted our ancestors.

The history of human vocations, according to Doctor William T. Harris, late United States commissioner of education, goes back to a time when men were miserable slaves whose total energies were required to wrest from nature their subsistence. There was a time when ninety-nine per cent of the men were absolutely compelled to struggle for food, which consisted largely of fish and game, or to manufacture rude clothing and other primary creature-comforts for themselves and those immediately dependent on them. To-day a large portion of the world's workers are adding the element of beauty to that which was primarily merely useful. Many others minister to the moral and intellectual wants of the race. **Man will be emancipated from the slavery of harsh industrial conditions some day, but not until human invention and power of combination shall reach the point where machinery can produce a plentifulness of the necessaries of life at a very low cost.** Then there will be less slavery, less intense devotion to pursuits that render men and women mere machines. When that day comes the race will demand more workmen of a high degree of culture in the higher vocations. In other words, the future human race, the type of man now in process of growth, will evolve some day into a more perfect being, a creature of more complex wants, and he will need the assistance of his fellows in esthetic pursuits for which there will be adequate remuneration. The improved race will demand more artists, more scientists, more musicians, and others, in complex and unforseen pursuits wherein they will serve the ends of culture. All the available nooks and crannies of nature will some day be explored by the new man, the man whose ancestors are now warped by narrow manual pursuits, who are now the mere grooms or attendants of machines, or of their more greedy and successful fellow men. These arts open the gates of a bright future, and promise to make men free; but a continual readjustment of vocations is in progress, and all laborers who are mere 'hands' must work at a continually growing disadvantage.

Dr. Harris puts the case in a forcible way, bringing his keen analysis to bear on the problem. According to him, the progress of the world in inventions necessitates a constant, and sometimes abrupt, ascent of mere hand labor into intelligent directive power.

Higher Vocations.

The ruder pursuits minister directly to the satisfaction of the wants of food and the coarser forms of clothing and shelter. The higher vocations relate to the satisfaction of man's spiritual wants, and the supply of means for luxury and amusement. The number of persons required in these higher spheres, especially in the production of articles of luxury and of ornamental goods, is increasing rapidly. In the United States and Great Britain five in a hundred laborers are actually pursuing vocations that have for their object the addition of ornament to what is already useful, or the direct ministration to culture in some form. When the ratio is reversed and only five in a hundred are needed to provide the crude necessary articles of consumption, and the remnant of society may devote itself to the higher order of occupations—then the economic problem will be solved.

The trend of social history, according to the eminent expounder of Hegel—Doctor Harris—now becomes apparent, in the light of man's destiny. It is not merely the emancipation of man from thralldom to nature. The plentiful supply of his material wants would be only a curse if there did not remain a high state of activity in the work for the spiritual perfection of man. In the civilization of to-morrow it is apparent that there will be a higher average of education, and a greater activity in the fields of honorable achievement along the lines of rational endeavor, than to-day. Without such exertion we should be no better than the lazy tribes of the tropics.

Everybody wants food, clothing, and other creature-comforts; all want articles of luxury, means of protection, and the ministry of culture, each in proportion to his degree of civilization. The new demands must call for services of the cultured along these higher lines.

Machinery a Blessing.

The more application of machinery the fewer laborers are needed in the departments where a narrow or special education will suffice, and the more the laborer is required to have a general and humane culture. **This doctrine contains the cheering gospel of final emancipation from drudgery.** The only condition attached to it is that all shall be educated, and this condition is indeed the best part of the gospel. It makes it the business of society and of every member of it to see that each and all are educated. It becomes the interest of the selfish man as well as the ideal of enlightened philanthropy **to have each member of society so intelligent that he can find his proper vocation,** his place of labor in the higher order of cultured human occupations. **To be able to do only by hand what a machine can do, is to be a pauper, is to work at a continually increasing disadvantage.** Invention makes obsolete the skill of previous generations—of immediately preceding years, even—and those who are too ignorant, too poor, or too old to readjust their employments and learn new trades are not able to earn a living.

Production Increases.

We are each year increasing our capacity as producers. **Machinery is manufacturing more and more of the things which supply man's manifold wants.** The manual-labor problem will be largely solved **when the majority shall be excused from the arts of production,** and when only a few persons, comparatively, shall be required in those manual handicrafts that create the ruder necessaries, which bring forth the products of everyday life. As before indicated, the world's workers will then be called into fields of greater intellectual and spiritual activity.

A few years ago we read of the destruction of this and that machine by angry peasants in Europe, and by farm laborers in America; yet there is no greater error abroad than the common one which assumes that machinery has supplanted human labor. Machinery is not the enemy of the laboring man. Its grand work has scarcely more than begun, yet it has brought many benefits to the laborer. It has already raised the scale of living, by decreasing the cost of manufactures, and it makes necessary the employment of far more workers than were employed before its advent. Countless thousands of men and women are now engaged in useful industries, **industries that were unknown before the era of machines.** Let us resort to facts: The census of the United States for 1880 shows that 185 per cent more people were employed in manufactures in 1880 than in 1850, and that they were employed at an increase of 300 per cent in wages. To be specific, there were 957,059 persons employed, in 1850, as against 2,732,595, in 1880. They received $236,-755,464, as wages, against $947,953,795, in 1880. During that era the population did not keep pace with the marvelous increase of wages, for it scarcely more than doubled.

Let any person who doubts these facts, or who fails to comprehend them in their abstract and somewhat repellant statistical form, consider some of the marked advances in the economic progress of the world. The revelations in this line are striking indeed. Almost every invention made in modern times has called for the manufacture of machinery, which, being completed, **has required a large number of mechanics to operate it. The world is full of trades formerly unknown, alive with the busy hum of marvelous industries unseen by our forefathers.** I submit a few of the trades that have benefited mankind by enlarging the sphere of activities for men and women alike, by giving employment to a vast army of workers. The reader will doubtless be able to add largely to my list, but the following outline shows how trades have been multiplying during a few generations: Chemical, nautical, and astronomical instruments, spinning and weaving of all kinds, from delicate fabrics of silk, et cetera, to carpets and heavier textiles, improvements in cutlery manufacture, fire-arms, musical instruments, steamboats, steamships, railroad trains and railroad machinery, paper manufactures of all kinds, marvelous printing and lithographing presses and machinery, telegraph and its allied industries, electrical machines, including telephones and phonographs, typewriting machines, gas machinery, clocks, many marvelous forms of the spinning jenny, power looms, bolt, nut, and nail works, wood-working machinery, great bridges and other structures of the new era, photography and allied arts, sewing machines, boot and shoe-making machines, infinite iron and metal processes, hydraulic and mining machinery, scores of agricultural inventions that have changed the face of nature—and thousands of machines that were absolutely undreamed of in the old days of ox teams and hand power.

It is a far cry from the days of beacon-lights on the hillsides of colonial America to the wireless telegraph on ships and mountains, from the pony express of our western frontier to the modern automobile and vestibuled railroad trains, but every turn of the great wheel of progress is along the lines indicated in the foregoing analysis.

PART II.

Fundamentals

OF

Street-car Control

BEING A DISCUSSION OF

The Legal and Economic Principles
of Public Service as Applied
to Rail Highways

—— BY ——

LEIGH H. IRVINE

CROWN PUBLISHING COMPANY
26 Clay Street
SAN FRANCISCO
— 1907 —

Reprinted from "SIXTY MILLION SLAVES," Copyright 1888, LEIGH H. IRVINE, and from the San Francisco Trade Journal, by permission of The Calkins Newspaper Syndicate.

EXPLANATORY.

This argument was made by me two decades ago, though the reader might be led to believe that it was inspired by the present street-car strike in San Francisco.

Twenty years ago, in Kansas City, Mo., I was a law partner of Frank P. Blair, now an eminent Chicago attorney. In connection with Mr. Blair and Judge Ashby, of Omaha, Nebraska, I made a thorough study of the railway problem in its legal and economic aspects. That study, then, pursued for more than two years, led me to conclude that ownership of the highway—the track itself—should be vested in the government, and that the **ownership and operation** of cars fall within the province of private industry. Inherently a highway, or **an exclusive franchise for its use**, should never be the subject of monopoly. The years intervening have served to confirm me in the opinion originally formed.

My views were set forth in detail in a series of lectures that were published in book form in 1888, under the title, "Sixty Million Slaves; a Lawyer's Plea for the People." Some economists and several public men of note indorsed the deductions as sound and practical, and the late M. J. Becker, chief civil engineer of the Panhandle System, pronounced the plan of a joint operation of trains over a public track a practical scheme; in fact, there were several companies operating over a long track near Columbus, Ohio, at the time, and each company was simply leasing the right of way over the road with the privilege of using it at specified times in conjunction with other companies.

The substance of the argument that follows is from "Sixty Million Slaves" and from an address delivered before the University Extension Club at Sacramento in 1898. As the discussion covers fundamental problems, it is, with some additions, apropos of the present situation in San Francisco.

LEIGH H. IRVINE.

26 Clay Street, San Francisco, May 20, 1907.

UNDER modern social conditions strikes, boycotts, lock-outs, and other economic diseases are multiplying with increasing frequency. Federations of labor on the one hand and great combinations of capital on the other discourage the middleman, disarrange industry, and plunge society into bitter strifes.

Though the courts originally regarded strikes as unlawful conspiracies they now grant not only the right to strike, but to employ pickets. One result of such decisions is that strikes are now conducted as great industrial wars, being directed by national commanders.

While these signs of social maladjustment multiply, the class struggle predicted and agitated by socialists seems to come closer every day. Thoughtful men who are neither millionaires, labor agitators, nor socialists naturally begin to ask where this strife is to end. The stern capitalist of courage may call for state militia or Federal troops when the public peace is overthrown, for example, during a street-car strike, and a president of the determination of a Cleveland, ignoring an Altgeld's gubernatorial protest, protects Chicago's street-cars by sending an escort of Uncle Sam's soldiers. Thereupon the socialists and the public ownership party demand municipal ownership, and with every new strike there is renewed discussion. Thousands of writers and speakers travel over the old roads that lead nowhere, and each outbreak finds the problem as far from solution as ever. Must the strife always continue? Must the remedy forever remain a mystery?

Not Socialism.

I agree with Professor Seligman, of Columbia University, that it is possible to advocate government ownership—especially municipal ownership—of some forms of property, without incurring the imputation of socialism; and if the right line of demarkation is drawn there is a field for public ownership, in co-operation with private industry in the operation of street-cars in cities. It is my purpose to analyze the question of public ownership as applied to the street-car problem, and to show that the public ownership of the highway itself, as distinguished from the public ownership and operation of the cars, is consistent with the modern system of industry, now conducted along the conservative and recognized lines of individualism. In other words, a city may justly own the iron highways within its territory, may also own the power plants by which cars are moved, and may charge track toll and power rentals to competing operating companies, all this without interfering with the rights of private capital, and without overthrowing the present economic system of industry. This distinction preserves the rights of all classes, and overcomes the objection that municipal operation would involve the hiring of a vast army of men.

It is now generally recognized by economists that government may "properly do what the private individual can not do, will not do, and ought not to do." [Seligman.] The private ownership of any kind of a highway, the exclusive use of that which of right belongs to the public, this comes fairly within the limitation of what private individuals and corporations ought not to do.

Railroads Are Highways.

The Supreme Court of the United States has decided several times, as have the supreme courts of many states, that railways are public highways. In the case of the Pensacola Telegraph Company (96 U. S., page 1), Chief Justice Waite held that government has the undoubted "power to make a government monopoly of the management of railways and the telegraph, and to appropriate to its use the existing lines of both."

Under the law of eminent domain private property must, under the compelling force of public demand, be surrendered, after just compensation, for the benefit of the majority. Every person who has ever seen a condemnation jury at work knows what may be accomplished when a railroad company, in its quasi public character, needs a man's farm for its switch yards.

In some of the earlier legal battles defendants who opposed the right of railways to condemn their lands argued that railroads were private ways because they were so operated that none but their owners could use them, and because every vehicle not owned by the company was barred from the railroad; but the courts have uniformly held that railroads are public highways whose privileges are granted for a time to companies, subject, always, to the superior rights of the public; and that if railroads do not exist by public necessity the titles by which the companies hold many of their franchises can be set aside as absolutely null and void. Judge Jere Black announced this doctrine with singular force and clearness.

Though the cases cited pertain largely to interstate railroads, the principle and the reasoning apply with even greater logic to the case of street railways in modern cities, where interruptions of traffic by the ill-arranged affairs of private owners inflict sharp and disastrous inconvenience and losses upon the public.

Highways Belong to All.

Highways are of great antiquity. They existed in ancient Egypt, in Peru, and in Ceylon, where they reached a high degree of perfection. In Judges we find accounts of highways and by-ways, and Rome's Via Aurelia and Flamminian Way are as famous as the military roads of Caesar's day. Alexander von Humboldt speaks of the marvelous roads of the Incas, mountain highways over the Andes, constructed by forgotten generations. But whether we read of ancient highways in India, or of those described in Exodus or in the annals of excavated Troy, or even of the appearance on the highway of the chariot built by Erichthonius at Athens 1486 years before Christ, we find one condition—that highways were always owned by the people, and from the earliest times (down to the invention of the railroad) both civilized and savage men have always guarded their highways from private ownership. Whether a bridlepath or a chariot way, the road always remained

the heritage of the multitude. Men of all races, in all ages, have had the right to pass and repass over the public thoroughfares, which have been open to men, women, and children whether walking, driving, or riding. Horses, mules, asses, oxen, camels, elephants, dromedaries, reindeer, Arctic dogs, and even African ostriches ridden by jet black owners, have been free to travel over the highway, as free as the snow-skaters of Lapland or Holland, as free as an Oriental palanquin bearer or a modern chauffeur racing through the highways of an American city. With the advent of railroads the public was ruled off the track. Then began our monopolies and our strikes, interrupting land locomotion with modern vehicles.

A study of the history of highways shows that a comprehensive definition characterizes them as such modifications of the surface of the earth as will enable it fitly to receive that vehicle furnished by the civilization of the era. The path of a nomad and the steel rails of a modern trolley system are inherently a free means of land locomotion. The franchises and special privileges granted to owners of steel highways mark the first overthrow of the right of the public to use the roads. It is interesting in this connection to note that the first charters issued to American railroads made it plain that the exclusive right to own and operate trains on the highways was denied. The selling of exclusive franchises was a later invention of the money kings who made the railroad era of modern civilization in America.

Public Must Own the Track.

The restoration of the highway to the public is the remedy for the evils that come from strikes, because the track is the key that enables the owners of street-car lines to lock out the public and dictate the terms under which men will be hired to operate cars. Take the track from the magnate, and the giant that makes it possible to block our commerce while he fights with unions is tied and helpless. Abolish private ownership of the rail highway, permit the operation of cars by competing companies, and the problem is solved.

It is clear by all the legal authorities that in temporarily abandoning their right to build railways the state governments merely delegate to their transient agents—the railway companies—the right to carry on a great public necessity. By parity of reasoning we may substitute city for state, street railway for steam railway, and argue that the frequency of strikes and the paralysis of industry by the stopping of street-car service justify the condemnation of the street-car tracks, wires, and power houses under the law of eminent domain. That step once taken nobody could ever again bar the public from its right of locomotion in modern vehicles, over modern highways.   Bancroft Library

The fact that private companies have bought our highways in almost every American city is an evidence that public officers have never clearly understood that cities might have declined to go into the business of operating street-cars and still have retained the absolute right to say who shall operate them, and that none shall prevent their operation so long as anybody owns a car. Even if it be deemed wise to limit the general use of tracks to one or two companies, the right to allow almost unrestricted access during emergencies should always be retained by the public.

The character of the railway is such as to make it impracticable for everybody to run his own vehicle thereon, but it is possible to permit a limited number of operating companies to compete over a track owned by the public; it is possible to say that no highway shall ever be sold to anybody or permitted to earn money for any corporation. To preserve the freedom of the masses the highways of every character must be as remote from private ownership as were the wagon roads over which the pioneers crossed the continent in '49. The track itself must forever remain free from the clutch of monopoly.

ENGRAVED
AND
PRINTED
BY
CALKINS
PUBLISHING
HOUSE
SAN FRANCISCO

Lightning Source UK Ltd.
Milton Keynes UK
UKHW020637250321
380972UK00005B/315